GROWING
DISGRACEFULLY

© Jane Jago 2019

You are old - 3

Elderly opinions - 12

Festive thinking - 17

I am old - 21

Ageing in poems - 38

Ageing in short fiction - 49

YOU ARE OLD

You are old so you shouldn't do that
You should only like knitting. And cats.
It shouldn't be you
With a brand-new tattoo
Making love on an old yoga mat

You are old, you should only drink tea
With a small finger quirked daintily
It shouldn't be you
With a brandy or two
And a pint of Bacardi or three

You are old so you should be demure
Your thoughts should be simple and pure
So how do you thrive
In the lowest of dives
Where cheap sex is the only allure

You are old, so you should never roam
Should be timid, and always at home
Wearing slippers and robe
Not trotting the globe
With only a toothbrush and comb

You are old, and that prompts me to ask
How certain events came to pass
How you got a gold fang
And a piercing that hangs
And a dragon tattooed on your ass

You are old. Let me give you a tip
Your body's too saggy to strip
It shouldn't be you
Showing off your tattoo
At the head of a mass skinny dip

You are old so you should be alone
And grateful if ever I phone
You should wait in for me
With crumpets and tea
So why are you never at home?

You are old so you shouldn't bedazzle
You should be both faded and frazzled
It shouldn't be you
With a Harley (brand new)
And a Swarovski Crystal vajazzle

You are old, let me just make it clear
That even your knitting is queer
You should knit baby clothes
To warm tiny toes
Not merkins in purple cashmere

You are old, and you are a disgrace
Should be modest and downcast of face
It is so deeply wrong
That you're wearing a thong
And a peephole in black silk and lace

You are old so you shouldn't do this
You should just rise above tell and kiss
But your feed on Twitter
Is funny and bitter
I think you're just taking the piss

You are old, tell me what could be worse
Than waiting in line for a hearse
You should live life in fear
Always wanting me near
Instead you just mock me in verse

You are old, so your favourite hue
Should be beige, or perhaps powder blue
But you dress like a harlot
In black lace, and scarlet
And skyscraper-heeled fuck me shoes

You are old, let me give you a clue
On the things you're too ancient to do
No clothes far too tight
Never party all night
And don't cuss till you turn the air blue

You are old, so at home is your place
Just counting the lines on your face
But you party all night
Crawling home when it's light
Your whole life is a bloody disgrace

You are old and your purse should be thin
You should live out of packets and tins
You should practice economy
Not waste cash on bonhomie
And you really should give up the gin

You are old, and that should be a sorrow
You should husband the time you have borrowed
Yet you fritter each day
As you laughingly say
What's the worry, it's never tomorrow

You are old and that can't be much fun
You should sit home and live like a nun
But you've pierced both your nipples
And you rode a Speed Triple
Round the Nurburgring clocking a ton

You are old and by all nature's laws
Father Time should be stretching his jaws
But you greet the hereafter
With welcoming laughter
Say it's not the end, just a pause

You are old, with your thread almost spun
You should look back on all you have done
Repenting your sins
As night marches in
But you're out on the town having fun

You are old, and you should be depleted
Modern techno should have you defeated
But you bought an iPhone
Never leave it alone
And I'm shocked by the filth that you tweeted

You are old, stop embarrassing me
By how badly behaved you can be
Just because you are able
To dance on the table
Don't do it where people can see

You are old, let there be no debate
You are well past your own sell by date
You have some things that sag
And some more things that bag
But you still seem to think life is great

You are old, don't you see it's too late
You can no longer procrastinate
But you're riding the sleeper
Towards the grim reaper
Still flicking two fingers at fate

You are old, so your idea of fun
Should involve cups of tea and a bun
It should not come to pass
That your wrinkly old ass
Is in Magaluf soaking the sun

You are old, let there be no dubiety
That the aged are a drain on society
You should spend your twilight
Being humbly polite
But you won't even practice sobriety

You are old, will you please act your age
Please be kindly, and simple, and sage
It shouldn't be you
At a quarter past two
Pole dancing on stage in a cage

You are old but that is no excuse
To be drunken and loud and so louche
I'm not posting the bail
To save your saggy tail
When you get yourself done for abuse

You are old, why are you not more calm?
Your should offer both succour and balm
Instead you just slight me
To rage you incite me
Without ever a trace of a qualm

You are old so you shouldn't wear that
You should only like shoes that are flat
You should never be seen
In stilettos, bright green
And a black leather biker-style hat

You are old, quite a lot needs a shave
Or a wax if you're terribly brave
While you're at it don't skip
The despised upper lip
You look like a moustachioed knave

You are old and your backside has spread
As have the grey hairs on your head
But you stick out your chest
Treat yourself to the best
Say, you'll bloody well live till you're dead

You are old, why are you not depressed
By the shortage of time you have left
Do you drink to forget
Or are you truly set
On meeting your fate half-undressed

You are old, and your winter is near
When cold winds will blow round your ears
When you'll shiver and shake
And your old bones will quake
Why doesn't that fill you with fear?

You are old, and your manners these days
Seem screwed up in every way
Last week on twitter
You called me a shitter
And on Facebook, you're turning me grey

You are old, you should truly act thus
Should be humble and not make a fuss
The award of a pension
Should add this dimension
But you just drink vodka. And cuss

You are old and you make me feel sad
Behaving like some drunken lad
Your lack of decorum
On Internet forums
Convinces me you have run mad

You are old and the grooves in your skin
Speak volumes of cigarettes and gin
But you feel no blame
Not one inkling of shame
At the outward display of your sins

You are old and your time you should treasure
Should be quietly husbanding leisure
Not wasting your days
In hedonist ways
And the casual grasping of pleasure

You are old, which would seem to suggest
That a quiet life should suit you best
But you're constantly out
And you racket about
Saying, when I am dead I can rest

ELDERLY OPINIONS

You are young, and you ought to take care
There are internet weirdos out there
That hunky young fellow
Who sounds cool and mellow
May be something less wholesome. Beware

When considering physical pleasure
There are very few things you can measure
Neither length, sir, nor girth
Is the measure of worth
It's the way that you use them, my treasure

I am quite old enough to be brave
And ask why the cover boys shave
I think that those bristles
Could make a girl whistle
And turn something happy quite grave

Said the girl with the basilisk stare
You just get your fist out of my hair
I don't mind a change
Or position that's strange
But you ain't putting that thing in there

I'm a woman who really likes. Shoes
And fit guys with iron-hard thews
And peach pie and custard
And hot dogs (with mustard)
And really big glasses of booze

When people ask are you a poet
I mostly say not as you know it
I rhyme to poke fun
And use verse like a gun
And if I find a belt, hit below it

You are young, but too adult for folly
You're as cold and as spiky as holly
With your head up your ass
And your youth fading fast
You may never find time to feel jolly

I'm a writer who don't have a muse
Just a pen. And a head full of blues
But don't don't take it to heart
For I'm just an old fart
Whose scribbles are fuelled by booze

I am old the unenviable fate
Of all those who pass through the gate
It's inevitable you
Will get saggy-assed too
And grow weeds in your lady estate

I am old, but my memory's fine
I can still smell the grass, taste the wine
Hear the song, touch the face
Find that private, warm place
Where love came and called the first time

A 'celebrity' thinks up a diet
And everyone dashes to try it
But you get best success
By just eating less
You don't need a book, so don't buy it

A beauty both gentle and soft
Was going to marry a toff
He wanted to spank her
She called him a wanker
And now the engagement is off

If you would catch a husband, they said
You must be compliant in bed
But once in the sack
He just lay on his back
So she made him a sandwich instead

You are young, but you've no time to play
Social media owns every day
You keep posting selfies
Although it's not healthy
Each one steals some spirit away

When it's Easter the bunny hops by
Bringing chocolate, for kiddies knee high
But mummy copes fine
If she has enough wine
To block out the sugar high cries

As we grow old together, he said
I feel happy and warm and well-fed
Though I have to reflect
That I didn't expect
False teeth in a glass by the bed

I just want a coffee, he said
And a sandwich of bacon and bread
I don't need a big list, or
A snarky barista
That stuff really does in my head

Mother swan hatched her cygnets today
They are tiny, and downy, and grey
Does the proud mum remember
That when it's December
Their daddy will chase them away

As we walk, there's a scent in the wind
That excites us. Enticing us in
With a hint of hot spice
Both exotic and nice...
It's a takeaway box by the bin

When beauty crept out of his bed
He cried, what's gotten into your head
Oh why give your heart
To that ugly old f**t
It's the depth of his wallet, she said

Being summer we could have such fun
Drinking icy cold beer in the sun
Or at rest in some glade
With a book in the shade
But no, you want to go for a run

When I was young and in my prime
I had to get to work on time
Dress up smartly fix my face
Comport myself with style and grace
But now I'm old and very flighty
I go shopping in my nightie

When you're young and a bit of a raver
You can get by on offering 'favours'
But a bosom that's slipped
And a hairy top lip
Are not things that guys want to savour

I am old and I'm thinking the sky
Is the same blue as my father's eyes
And I wonder if he
Will be smiling at me
When I finally say my goodbyes

Please tell me what jogging achieves
Apart from a pain in the knees
It jiggles your bits
From the bum to the tits
And it makes you go purple and wheeze

FESTIVE THINKING

I am old, old enough to remember
When Christmas began in December
When in January
Naught was left of the tree
But a bonfire, with bright glowing embers

I am old and I'm not feeling festive
All this jollity makes me quite restive
Can we please just remember
It's early December
And stop being Yuletide suggestive

I am old and I'm already bored
With carols and praising the lord
I'm fed up with holly
I'm not feeling jolly
I think I may just go abroad

I am old and my patience is thin
Bloody Christmas gets under my skin
I don't like rum punch
Or turkey for lunch
Or them toffees you get in a tin

I am old, and I just like to say
That Christmas is one or two days
Its one saving grace
Is it takes little space
And I'm whistling till it goes away

I am old and I looked out last night
On a landscape of sparkling lights
Which shone through the rain
And entered my brain
As a feeling of pre-Yuletide blight

I am old, and I have a disorder
It's the fear of the festive defrauder
Who sings you some verse
Whilst denuding your purse
Look out. It's the Christmas marauder

I am old and I'd like to remind you
That most of your childhood's behind you
If a fat bloke in red
Sits on your bed
He's really not there to be kind to you

I am old and I've done some festivity
And attended the odd school nativity
But I'd much rather be
At home with just me
Being jolly destroys creativity

I am old and I can't help but wonder
Why Christmas tears families asunder
It seems all about greed
And society's need
For the childish acquiring of plunder

The countdown to Christmas is here
Which I watch with diminishing cheer
I fear for humanity
But hang on to my sanity
By consuming both brandy and beer

Deck the house with chains of paper
Nah, nah, nah, nah, nah, nah, nah, nah, nah
Clout the kids and cut a caper
Nah, nah etc
Fill the socks up
Drain the money
Nah, nah, nah, nah, nah, nah, nah, nah, nah
January isn't funny
Nah, nah etc

It is Christmas, and to ensure cheer
It is necessary to buy beer
A turkey with thighs
Of inordinate size
And enough sweets to make you feel queer

I don't dislike Christmas per se
If it doesn't last too many days
That's none in November
And three in December
Then please put the tinsel away

When your friends wait with stars in their eyes
For the present their loved one will buy
Their dream is precise
So boys, take this advice
That gas station flowers won't fly

I AM OLD

I am old, and that hat really fits
I have wrinkles and saggy old bits
But I live every day
And I'd just like to say
That your misery gets on my tits

I am old, I can tell that you fear
The passing of days and of years
But this grasping at youth
Fails to see the real truth
We should make time for pretzels and beer

I am old, I can see your mistakes
And your attitudes make my teeth ache
Try admitting fault
Like a thinking adult
Please don't sulk like a special snowflake

I am old I have noticed this fact
There's no need to approach it with tact
I don't bother that you
Will have noticed it too
But stop smirking or you will get smacked

I am old and I couldn't care less
If my attitude causes distress
I won't stop the booze
Or wear sensible shoes
And your moaning just bores me to death

I am old, why do you ask me questions
And make those impertinent suggestions?
I will not age with grace
So stop pulling that face
And be off, you disturb my digestion

I am old, that's no bone of contention
And I got here without intervention
So why would i think twice
On your so-called advice?
Hush your mouth, I'm not paying attention

I am old and I really don't care
If I'm wrinkled and grey in the hair
I don't care if you slight me
But don't try to fight me
I'll still whop your ass if you dare

I am old, so just please give me room
And stop handing me your doom and gloom
You are just such a bore
And I've heard it before
Can't you put on a less mournful tune

I am old, which in turn makes me proof
Against all of the follies of youth
I don't think that the net
Is the coolest place yet
Or that reading it makes it the truth

I am old now, and as my days pass
I find I can no longer be arsed
To try to conform
And act uniform
Might as well be a sheep and eat grass

I am old as you rightly suggest
And often I don't look at my best
But I just think sod that
And shove on a hat
And stick out my oversized chest

I am old and I really don't mind
The sprinkle of grey, or the lines
And I have no misgivings
About my way of living
Having fun really isn't a crime

I am old and I'm finding it strange
That you watch me like I was deranged
But I still have my wits
And some functioning bits
So please leave me alone for a change

I am old, and I'd just like to say
That I have little time for delay
You may wish to note
That I've time by the throat
And I'm bloody well living each day

Come on gran, Carpe Diem they said
But the pillow is soft to my head
I have doughnuts and milk
And my jammies are silk
So, f**k it, I'm staying in bed

I am old, and I couldn't care less
About how you believe I should dress
I may step out in leather
Or a fan made of feathers
Or my underwear's silky caress

I am old so I have to expect
The occasional pain in the neck
A bladder that leaks
The occasional creak
And a face that's a wrinkly old wreck

I am old, and that is my excuse
For subjecting my liver to abuse
I've an appetite for gin
A digestion of tin
And a belly that likes to hang loose

I am old and I'm not in the mood
For pompous young eejits like you
I don't want to hear
About bloody craft beer
And I'm really not eating tofu

I am old, and I don't give a shit
About gravity's work on my bits
I'm not some humble dame
Who can be 'body shamed'
By a halfwit with silicone tits

I am old, I don't need an excuse
For refusing to be a recluse
Almost any old night
I might grab me a bite
I don't care if I'm thought to be loose

I am old and I have no illusions
I have not yet succumbed to confusion
But when you ask me 'why?'
I can see in your eye
That you think me the prey of delusion

I am old, and I'd quite like to mention
That age adds a certain dimension
It becomes very clear
That there's little to fear
Outside of one's own inner tensions

I am old, and today my bones ache
And I'm sloughing my skin like a snake
My wrinkles are saggy
My arse very baggy
I think I'll just stay home and bake

I am old, but the time I shall take
To cure you of youth's worst mistake
In all of life's mess
You will find no distress
Is so deep as to not cure with cake

I am old, and that means I'm allowed
To lead, and not follow the crowd
I am happy and fit
And I don't give a shit
I'm myself and that just makes me proud

I am old and my wrinkles and sags
Make me look like a used paper bag
And the state of my belly
Like strawberry jelly
Hangs over my trousering rags

I am old and I like to wear jeans
But skinny ones make me feel mean
And as for the flare
I'd sooner go bare
Why is there nothing between

I am old and it is my intention
To firmly resist intervention
I'm sure you mean well
But my life would be hell
If I took your advice on abstention

I am old, also lazy and fat
With the morals of some alley cat
My clothes are a squeeze
And I have dodgy knees
But I don't give a bugger for that

I am old, and I have some advice
When you slip on life's patches of ice
Do not sit and blub
Take yourself to the pub
And order a large something nice

I am old and I find it amusing
That this body I'm busy abusing
Has lasted these years
Through the fags and the beers
Without diet or exercise using

I am old, which to me indicates
A perfectly wonderful state
In which no-one but me
Says how I ought to be
And I've no need for doubting or hate

I am old, which means I get to choose
My friends, and my food, and my booze
I don't need advice
About what is nice
At my age I have f**k all to lose

I am old and I'm not too impressed
By the way you expect me to dress
If I have my hair blue
Which I really might do
It won't be the shade you suggest

I am old and your arguments bore me
Coz you really don't need to think for me
I've done seven decades
With none of your aid
So be off, lest you unleash the sore me

I am old and I have an admission
That I'm seriously lacking ambition
Except, I must say
To awaken each day
Which occasionally comes to fruition

I am old, and I don't like the rain
As it rattles the glass in its frame
And I'm not fond of fog
And nor is the dog
As the water gets into our brain

I am old and you may know I write
I do all things, from novels to bites
Of fiction and verse
Some's bad some is worse
And some may well keep you up nights

I am old, let me make one thing clear
That no matter what time of the year
There never will be
Any sort of 'new' me
I'm fond of the old one. And beer

Though I'm old, I can still dance the dance
I can still feel the thrill of romance
And I yet know the bliss
Of a cuddle and kiss
And of nookie, when I get the chance

Though I'm old, I am not such a fool
As much of the modern gene pool
I don't need to be told
That ice will be cold
Or detergent's not food as a rule

I am old, thank you for your concern
But it's okay, I have time to burn
I don't reminisce
Though I do take the piss
That's a skill you might quite like to learn

I am old. It's a natural state
It's what everyone has on their plate
Even in life's December
Keep fanning the embers
The alternative just ain't so great

I am old, and I'm letting life slide
Unashamed that my ass is so wide
That from April to June
It blocks out the moon
And it has an effect on the tides

I am old, just in case you can't see
But there's still no-one I'd rather be
I'm fat and I'm funny
Love people, not money
And mostly I love being me

I am old and my needs are quite small
I will just make a list of them all
A home of my own
An iPad and phone
And a man with a good set of balls

I am old, and the hands of the clock
My efforts at youthfulness mock
Though young men can find
I look good from behind
When they look at the front it's a shock

I am old, and today I lunched well
As my squiffy legged progress might tell
For the bottle of wine
That looked really fine
Is gone - nothing left but the smell

Being old is like getting permission
To be feckless and not feel contrition
One can wear a red hat
Get six dogs and a cat
And pour scorn on the words of physicians

I am old, but f**k ageing with grace
That's an idea I'll never embrace
I shall live till I die
With a glint in my eye
And a sarcastic grin in my face

I am old, and my friends are old too
But we still act like we used to do
We still have that wiggle
Are still prone to giggles
And still like a bevy. Or two

I am old and my wrinkly old face
Tells tales of a life lived at pace
Each laugh and each tear
Has left its mark here
As has every slap and embrace

I am old, which surprises me slightly
Though it's better than I thought it might be
There are days in the sun
Irresponsible fun
And no need for behaving politely

I am old and my bosoms now sag
I could carry them round in a bag
They're now far from my face
Very close to my waist
Where they hang like a tattered old flag

I am old, but my saggy old ass
Isn't ready to go out to grass
I will just give a miss
To rooms smelling of piss
And tonic wine by the small glass

I am old, in my youth I was fine
But I'm somewhat corroded by time
I've been battered it's clear
By chocolate and beer
Not to mention the gin. And the wine

I am old, and I find the condition
Akin to a war of attrition
As all of my bits
From my bum to my t*ts
Seem determined to head for perdition

I am old, but not wrinkled or sweet
Not a granny who's neat and petite
I am outsize and proud
Correspondingly loud
In the kitchen enjoying the heat

I am old, which I find quite a lark
And with every year that I mark
I shall just try to do
Something I'm told not to
Like playing nude bowls in the park

I am old, and I guess you might say
That I'm now in the shortening days
Which is why I intend
To live right to the end
I'll wear out before I rust away

I am old, but I don't mind a bit
I'm unbothered by saggy old t**s
I don't care if my face
Is a wrinkly disgrace
Though it's sad that my skin doesn't fit

I am old and increasingly crusty
My corners are now getting dusty
I am like an old book
Wherein you'd like to look
Except that it smells rather musty

I am old, should I need an excuse
For allowing my bits to hang loose
Without garments elastic
The freedom's fantastic
Though my look gets a bit of abuse

I am old, and I worship the sun
A snooze in the heat is such fun
I lay like a lizard
With a sign on my gizzard
'Turn me over when you think I'm done'

I am old, but I have to confess
That grownup stuff makes me depressed
I'm so not a girl
For twinset and pearls
I wear jeans and I don't own a dress

I am old, but I still have my wits
And most of my pertinent bits
And when I see it's true
That I scandalise you
I can still laugh myself into fits

I am old, and the purpose of clothes
Is to cover the sags and the holes
Pursuing of fashion
Is wasting your passion
While stylists just get up my nose

I am old, and I'm down on my knees
Checking the dog's fur for fleas
With a comb and a spray
I've been down here all day
Will you give me a hand up now, please?

There are times when old age is the pits
When it totally lacks pleasant bits
It does in your head
When you roll out of bed
And promptly trip over your tits

Now I'm old people ask my advice
Thinking wisdom to be beyond price
But they never bring gin
Or big cakes in a tin
So. Why should I be arsed to be nice?

Being old means I'm quite without shame
I can swear, belch and f**t without blame
I can drink till I'm squiffy
Make jokes that are iffy
And call all my neighbours rude name

I am old, of which there's no debate
Being wrinkly and rumpled's my fate
Lost control of my bits
And the left of my tits
Now hangs down twice as low as its mate

I am old, and incredibly rude
I like humour that's lusty and lewd
So just pass me a beer
Then pretend I'm not here
But don't get between me and food

The man with the camera said
You are old, so you ought to be dead
You have titties that sag
And a face like a ball bag
So I punched him up side of his head

I have just seen my backside in shorts
And it's almost as bad as I thought
It's as broad is a ship
And my bum cheeks have slipped
Those are hips built for sitting, not sport

I am old, and the young think me rude
Because I laugh really loud and throw food
I am never PC
And I never drink tea
But I do like to swim in the nude

I am old, and persistent abuse
Has rendered my skin somewhat loose
So it shouldn't be news
That it's made my tattoos
Grow misshapen and blurred

I am old, if you take my advice
You won't waste time on being thought 'nice'
No dear, what gets my vote
Is grab life by the throat
Never worry about thinking twice

AGEING IN POEMS

FRIENDSHIP

Happy birthday to my friend
We've seen some years slip past
And sometime it's a source of pain
How time goes by so fast
When did wrinkles colonise
The skin around our sparkling eyes
When did we grow not young
When did grey invade our hair
Yesterday it wasn't there
But we're still up for fun
Outside I guess we aren't the girls
We always used to be
But underneath we're just as daft
And you're still young to me

COUNTRY SONG

Sitting alone at the bar, remembering when I was fine
I used to be a beauty then, before the claws of time
Sitting with my pal Jim Beam, the memories they linger
Unlike money, cars and men, that slip right through my fingers

Looking back to when my chest was neat and tight and perky
When my skin was more like silk and less like frozen turkey
Looking back to when I had the perfect little ass
Back when I was seventeen, half a century past

Sitting alone at the bar, while the juke box plays old tunes
Songs they sung when I was young, not a wrinkled prune
Sitting with an empty glass, staring at the wall
Remembering when I was young and John Boy he was tall

Looking back to when my chest was neat and tight and perky
When my skin was more like silk and less like frozen turkey
Looking back to when I had the perfect little ass
Back when I was seventeen, half a century past

Sitting alone at the bar with no one to stand me a beer
Where the hell did I go wrong to wind up sitting here

Sitting alone at the bar too drunk to get up and go home
Even the faithful dog has buggered off and left me alone

Looking back to when my life was all in front of me
Back to when I knew I could be what I dreamed I'd be
Looking back to when I had the world beneath my feet
Back when I was seventeen, and life was truly sweet

CRUEL ELD

Age has dropped a wrinkle here
And splashed a brown spot there
It's put some flaps beneath my arms
And made my chin grow hairs
As my skin has thinned and dried
My ass has gotten fatter
Fortunately age has taught
That that shit doesn't matter
As long as I have eyes to see
And still a heart to feel
I can ignore the signs of eld
And keep it strong and real
It is my wish to dance and sing
To spend and never save
To love and eat, and drink too much
Go laughing to my grave

GRANNY DANCING

Gran is at a discotheque
See her bump and grind
You must admit she really looks
Quite sexy. From behind
Gran is at a discotheque
Gyrating with delight
A man creeps up and slaps her ass
She turns. He gets a fright

INCONTINENCE KNICKERS

I don't need incontinence knickers
My bladder's surprisingly tight
And I don't want to plan out my funeral
When I see my future as bright
Don't call and expect me to tell you
My pin and identification
And it isn't yet quite time to mash my food
As an aid to mastication
You don't need to tell me to put on a coat
When I go out in the frost
I'm still on the bridge of my own little boat
And none of my marbles are lost
I don't need incontinence knickers
Or an over sixties plan
All I require is a drinkie or two
And the love of a grumpy old man

JUST AROUND THE BEND

I wonder where you really went
On your last mortal day
The day you left your aged shell
Just simply walked away
I can't believe you are no more
Your spirit shone so bright
I used to think that in this world
You were my guiding light
I miss your voice, I miss your laugh
I miss your steadying hand
Sometimes in sleep I hear you speak
From some far fabled land
And in my dreams you comfort me
Explain there is no end
You promise that you'll wait for me
Just around the bend

LOOSE SKIN

When I was young my skin did fit
But now it's stretched and sags a bit
And honestly I'm not too pleased
To find my boobs down by my knees
Beneath my arms there are some things
That people know as bingo wings
And this ignores my droopy ass
And teeth that live all night in glass
I really think I'd have the blues
Were it not for cake. And booze

TOGETHER

It's been a few years together
And we've picked up some shite on the way
We have weathered all sorts of weather
We've seen blue skies and black skies and grey
We've had the odd trouble along the road
And some pretty spectacular fights
But I wouldn't swap you for your weight in gold
Even though that sounds awfully trite
We can number our wrinkles one by one
And the white strands in our hair
But no one can take away the fun
Or the way you have always been there
I guess you know what I would say
If push turned into shove
We've had some lovely nights and days
And you've always been my love

MY FACE

My face in the cold light of morning looks
Creased and deeply bemused
Like the crumpled leaves of a very old book
A novel that's been harshly used
Like a discarded paper bag
Or an unwanted Christmas gift
The years have caused the skin to sag
But the fear of the needle precludes a lift
My chins in the morning number
Three and sometimes four
As into the bathroom I lumber
And lean against the hard door
Refusing to look at my reflection
I step into the shower
Where the comfort of steam and recollection
Gets me through this hour
I know how my face in the morning appears
But not for the rest of the day
I have been practicing all of these years
Just keeping my eyes turned away

OLD WOMAN

Her skin is like an autumn leaf
Delicate, crumpled dry
Her hair as soft as thistledown
When the wind blows it by
Her eyes, though blue, have faded now
No longer snapping bright
Her hands, lay folded in her lap
So thin they let in light
But still she smiles, and still she laughs
And still has time for friends
I watch, amazed, her courage
As she faces her life's end

AGEING IN SHORT FICTION

SANCTUARY

Two people are watching a flickering black and white television in a room lit only by the flames of a roaring log fire. They are sitting on a comfortable settee with the remains of a fish and chip supper on the low table in front of them. The woman feeds the remnants of her fish to a collie dog with one blue eye and one brown eye before rolling up the newspaper parcels and throwing them into the back of the fire.

"There," she says comfortably, "dishes done".

Her companion laughs, then leans over to plant a kiss on her smiling mouth.

"I never knew how much fun life could be."

She pats his face, but says nothing. The dog, however, appears to endorse his sentiments as it stands up and wags its plumy tail.

"You want out?" he asks and the tail wags harder.

Outside it is bitterly cold, and the moonlight picks out trees whose branches are laden with ice. The man waits on the wide porch as the dog quickly does whatever is necessary before dashing back to where there is a promise of warmth. He bends to stroke the silky head and they slip back indoors together. His companion has moved to the kitchen end of the big homely room and is heating something on top of the wood-burning stove.

"Hot chocolate."

The man grins, and runs a hand down her ample buttocks in appreciation.

"If you are going to get touchy-feely."

She removes the pan from the heat and turns into his embrace.

A goodish while later they are back in the comfortable embrace of the settee and the television is back on. They are idly watching the news, and contemplating bed, when a story catches their collective eye.

"Major General, Sir Sidney Wotheringham has now been missing for seven days, and concerns for his welfare are growing. Sir Sidney, who is believed to be suffering from a brain complaint similar to Alzheimer's Disease, left the hospital where he has lived for the past five months on the morning of Monday last. Staff assumed he was going for his usual bicycle ride." The newsreader lowers her voice and screws up her face to much the shape and texture of a prune. "He has not been seen since. His bicycle was found near junction twenty-five of the motorway. But Sir Sidney has vanished without a trace."

There is much more in this vein, as the missing man's son speaks on camera about the family's worry and their hope that his father is alive and well somewhere. The son looks into the eye of the camera with all the practised bonhomie of the career diplomat although he is as smooth and cold as marble, from his neatly clipped moustache to his gold cufflinks and his old school tie. He speaks of care and concern for his missing father but it looks to the two people watching the flickering screen as if he is only going through the motions for the look of things. The piece ends with a picture of an upright soldierly gentleman riding an equally upright bicycle.

The man on the settee snorts then grins and his companion takes his hand in both of hers.

"It's an awful shame to think of that poor old soldier out there in the coldest winter we have had for a decade," he says softly.

"Never mind, love, perhaps somebody has taken him in."

The man kisses her hand and goes to stand in front of a mirror which hangs on the wall beside the fireplace. He studies his bearded reflection and thinks how different he already looks from the sad soldier on his bicycle...

PERFECT

The Master Stonemason was in his eightieth summer and he was all but blind, still his hands knew their work and each chisel stroke was as clean and precise as it had been in his youth. Once he had cut and carved he began the laborious task of polishing, trusting nothing to the hands of his sons, or his grandsons, or the apprentices who watched in something like awe. When one of his sons would have intervened to help the old man, his only surviving daughter stepped in front of her brother.

"Leave him. Let him make his last work as glorious as his first."

When the last letter was incised and the last square inch of the finest Carrera marble was polished to a soft pure shine, the old man lifted his eyes to the sky and rested at last.

One by one, each man in the yard stepped up and laid a gentle hand on this thing of beauty the old man had crafted.

Last forward was the Master's daughter. Her homely features were shaped into the tenderest of smiles and she laid her cheek against the cool marble.

"It is perfect," she said softly, "now come home to your dinner".

The old man took her proffered hand and they walked away together - leaving the young men to carry the headstone the Master had created to its place on the grave of his beloved wife.

THE OLD ONE

It was cold by the window, and the old one moved to a winged armchair beside the roaring fire. With his brown woollen gown, and his scrawny neck, and his head sunk into his shoulders, he resembled nothing so much as a tortoise - and a bad-tempered one of those.

"Are you sure you are all right with this?" The voice was young enough to still be falling between baritone and treble, and the speaker was tall, and long-boned, and well muscled, and golden of skin, hair and eyes.

The old one's smile showed a mouthful of long yellowish teeth, although it seemed a genuine enough expression of amusement.

"Of course I'm all right with it. I'm old. I'm tired. I'm fed up. It's time somebody else stood at that window."

The youngster swallowed nervously.

"It's just a watching brief isn't it? They said... I mean... I understood..."

He lost himself in a morass if half sentences, and the old one laughed - a high cackle that somehow set the teeth on edge.

"Oh yes. All you will ever do is watch. The problem is there will, doubtless, be plenty of things you don't want to see."

"So I understand. I will learn to endure."

"You will indeed," the voice was dry, but not unkind. "I have a little time left here, so shall we watch together for a while."

"That would be a kindness," the youngster's voice was filled with the trepidation he hadn't known he felt until this moment.

To his surprise, the old one extended a leathery claw. He placed his young, strong hand around the yellowed and skinny fist, but, strangely, it seemed that he was drawing strength from the physical weakness of the oldster who he could almost fancy was diminishing before his eyes.

They went and stood in front of the huge pane of glass, and at first the young one could see nothing, but slowly his eyes became accustomed to the work and he could see. He saw cities and villages, grandfathers and newborns, horses and spacecraft. All of the world, he thought, was passing beneath his gaze and he could see every good deed, and observe every act of malice. He felt as if a heavy weight landed on his chest and had it not been for the dry strength of the old one he thought he might have fallen to the floor in a dead faint. The skinny old man passed a palsied hand across the glass and the moving panorama was replaced by the dark promontory on which the tower with its tall window stood.

As they watched, the cloud lifted, and a single shaft of moonlight pierced the gloom. Somewhere far away a click began striking.

As the twelfth chime of the bell sounded, the old one melted away leaving a pile of clothes and a faint aroma of decay.

The fresh young year leaned his forehead against the cold glass and drew a deep breath before opening his mind to the sorrows of the world.

BEING 95

Although I know I'm lucky, being ninety-five still sucks. Sure I still have my wits about me and I manage perfectly well in this little house. But I'm lonely. Not the not seeing people sort of lonely, the watching all your friends die sort.

Last night I dreamed of my beloved Alfie. He's been gone thirty years now, and I don't know why I asked him what he thought of the skinny bag of bones I've become.

He grinned and hugged me.

"You always were a bag of bones..."

And that's the most comfort I've had since he died.

ENLIGHTENMENT

She sat outside her cave. Her face was as seamed as the striated rocks behind her, and grime was ingrained into every crusty crack.

But still they came.

The rich, the famous, the desperate, all seeking enlightened words. To some she vouchsafed nothing and they crept away, ashamed. To others she gave but one word of hope. The third group bathed in the almost sightless seeming whiteness of her eyes and heard her words of wisdom.

When the last named supplicant backed away, she plugged her iPhone into its solar charger and offered a silent prayer of thanks for Google.

OLD HANDS

When she was a girl she had been vain about her smooth, white hands. After she married, she was proud of the tenderness of those hands as they cared for her babies. Once her children were grown she prided herself on the things her busy hands created - from baking and preserving to sewing and weaving.

Now she was an old woman her hands were twisted and knotted, although they still cooked and cleaned and cared.

She frowned at the papery skin.

Her husband caught the direction of her glance.

"I like your hands," he smiled, "they show you have lived."

POPPIES AND MEMORY

Lucie found Granddad in the garden. He was sitting on the bench opposite a bed of scarlet poppies. There were tears running down his seamed, brown cheeks.

Lucie scrambled into his lap.

"Aw Gramps, doncha cry."

The old man hugged her.

"Not really crying lovely. More remembering. There was poppies like them when we went back to the battlefields to do the decent thing by the bones of the dead."

Lucie thought for a moment then climbed down, and touched a flower with a gentle finger.

"You have to remember," she said slowly, "but they wouldn't want you to cry."

Printed in Great Britain
by Amazon